SERVING IN
CHURCH VISITATION

OTHER TITLES IN THE ZONDERVAN PRACTICAL MINISTRY GUIDE SERIES

Paul E. Engle is an executive editor and associate publisher for editorial development at Zondervan. He has served as a pastor and as an instructor in several seminaries. Among the eight books he has written are *Baker's Wedding Handbook, Baker's Funeral Handbook,* and *God's Answers for Life's Needs.*

Jerry M. Stubblefield served as chair of the Christian education department at Golden Gate Baptist Theological Seminary. He has experience as a pastor, campus minister, minister of education, denominational worker, and teacher at seminaries in Africa and Southeast Asia. He is the author of *The Effective Minister of Education.*

ZONDERVAN
PRACTICAL
MINISTRY GUIDES

SERVING IN CHURCH VISITATION

PAUL E. ENGLE, SERIES EDITOR
JERRY M. STUBBLEFIELD

GRAND RAPIDS, MICHIGAN 49530 USA

We want to hear from you. Please send your comments about this book to us in care of the address below. Thank you.

ZONDERVAN™

Serving in Church Visitation
Copyright © 2002 by Jerry M. Stubblefield

Requests for information should be addressed to:

Zondervan, *Grand Rapids, Michigan 49530*

Library of Congress Cataloging-in-Publication Data

Stubblefield, Jerry M., 1936–
    Serving in church visitation / Jerry M. Stubblefield.
       p.   cm. — (Zondervan practical ministry guides)
    Includes bibliographical references.
    ISBN 0-310-24103-0
    1. Visitations (church work). I. Title.   II. Series.
  BV4320 .S79 2002
  253'.7—dc21

                                           2002010999

Interior design by Sherri Hoffman

Printed in the United States of America

---

03 04 05 06 07 08 /❖ DC/ 10 9 8 7 6 5 4 3

CONTENTS

108722

HOW TO USE THIS GUIDE

Serving in Church Visitation is written for the experienced church visitor, as well as for those considering becoming a church visitor for the first time. The guide can be studied individually or in group settings. Its primary purpose is to provide encouragement to faithful church visitors and church staff members who take time from busy schedules to reach out to people who have needs in their communities. They participate in visitation because growing churches have effective visitation ministries. Not all visitation programs look alike, but each should be custom-built to fit particular local situations.

Serving in Church Visitation is designed as a study guide for church training classes where ideas are discussed and local strategies and procedures developed. Individuals should read the chapters prior to the group or class meeting. The content and application of the material can be expanded by using the discussion questions at the end of each chapter.

My prayer is that you and your church will have an effective church visitation ministry. May the Lord richly bless and use you, whether you are a lay member or a church staff member, as you serve in Christ's church by reaching out to people in need through the high calling of church visitation ministry.

—Jerry M. Stubblefield

ONE

Be Motivated: How Does the Bible Model the Importance of Visitation?

It was a cool and sunny February Sunday afternoon. I was helping Bethel Church do a community ministry survey. My visiting partner was Paul, a middle-aged man, and our assignment was to discover any needs community residents had that the church might meet. On that Sunday afternoon Paul and I found most people home, and we were received rather well. As we chatted about the information gathered and some of the things we thought that the church might do to minister to these people, we approached the last house in our assigned territory.

As we knocked on the door, we could hear noises coming from inside the house, but no one answered. We began to wonder if anyone would respond. Finally we heard a woman's voice call out, "Who is it?" "Paul and Jerry from Bethel Church," we replied. "We were just wondering if we could get some information from you." She opened the door, holding a four-year-old child who was limp in her arms. "I've been praying all day that someone would come who could help me with my sick daughter." She then told us that the girl had been running a fever for two days but that she was worse today. Her husband was a long-distance truck driver, due home any time, but she had no way to contact him. She had run out of money and didn't know what to do.

Paul and I assured her that we would help get medical care for her daughter. Our community ministry survey now seemed unimportant in light of the opportunity to meet an urgent immediate need. We took her to a nearby hospital emergency room that would treat her daughter and allow her to pay later. We stayed until the medical personnel had completed their treatment, and then we took mother and daughter back to their home.

As Paul and I drove back to church we agreed that, although we had set out to conduct a community ministry survey, God had given us the unexpected privilege of engaging in on-the-spot ministry. We thanked God for this opportunity to minister to the woman and her daughter.

The next morning I called the woman to see how her daughter was doing. Her husband, who had arrived during the night, answered the telephone. He reported that the medicine was working and that the little girl's fever had broken. She was expected to make a complete recovery in a few days. He said we'd been an answer to prayer by showing up at such a critical time of need. When I called Paul and shared the news, we prayed together, thanking God that we could be his chosen instruments to meet this family's need.

A few days later Paul and his wife visited this family and told them about Bethel Church and about the ways they thought that the church could meet their needs. It wasn't long before they visited Bethel Church. This incident illustrates just one of many forms church visitation can take.

Most Christians want to be sure that what they do is based on Scripture and follows biblical models. The Bible is filled with visitation examples. God himself made visits; angels visited people; the prophets went directly to people; and Jesus practiced visitation as he went to special events, walked along

BE MOTIVATED: How Does the Bible Model the Importance of Visitation?

11

the roads, and went to homes. The apostle Paul was a frequent visitor as he spread the gospel message on his missionary journeys. Peter visited in the homes of Cornelius and Dorcas. The list could go on and on.

Visitation is an ancient practice going back to the times recorded in the book of Genesis and running throughout Scripture. I'll highlight several Bible characters who practiced visitation and then show why they did it. These biblical characters illustrate principles that apply today as we engage in visitation. I trust that this will motivate you as you realize how important the idea of visitation is for God's people right now.

JESUS' COMMISSION

Matthew 28:18–20 has been called the Great Commission because it directs the people of God to be active in visitation and in disciple making:

> Then Jesus came to them and said, "All authority in heaven and on earth has been given to me. Therefore go and make disciples of all nations, baptizing them in the name of the Father and of the Son and of the Holy Spirit, and teaching them to obey everything I have commanded you. And surely I am with you always, to the very end of the age."

Visitation is not just a weekly church activity, nor is it an activity that Christians do through their own strength and ingenuity. Making contacts for Christ is serious business that requires us to visit in the same spirit Christ had, seeking his blessing and power for this significant endeavor. As Christians we can go out, knowing that Christ's authority goes with us and that he will be with us always, even to the very end of time.

Mark 16:15, a briefer version of the Great Commission, states, "[Jesus] said to them, 'Go into all the world and preach the good news to all creation.'" In some ways Mark is more specific, insofar as the Christian is commanded to go into all the world and preach—to share the good news of Jesus Christ with everyone.

VISITATION ESTABLISHED BY GOD

God visited Adam and Eve in the Garden of Eden both before and after their fall into sin:

> The LORD God took the man and put him in the Garden of Eden to work it and take care of it. And the LORD God commanded the man, "You are free to eat from any tree in the garden; but you must not eat from the tree of the knowledge of good and evil, for when you eat of it you will surely die."   Genesis 2:15–17

God personally placed Adam in the Garden of Eden to work and take care of it. God spent time with Adam there and saw that he needed a helper, so God created the woman, Eve. After this first couple had eaten the forbidden fruit from the tree of the knowledge of good and evil, God once again visited them in the Garden of Eden:

> Then the man and his wife heard the sound of the LORD God as he was walking in the garden in the cool of the day, and they hid from the LORD God among the

BE MOTIVATED: How Does the Bible Model the Importance of Visitation?

13

trees of the garden. But the L ORD God called to the man, "Where are you?"

He answered, "I heard you in the garden, and I was afraid because I was naked; so I hid."

And he said, "Who told you that you were naked? Have you eaten from the tree that I commanded you not to eat from?"   Genesis 3:8–11

This wasn't the first time God had visited with Adam and Eve in the garden. He was such a frequent visitor that they knew the sound of his footsteps. So at the beginning of human history, God himself modeled the practice of face-to-face inter-action with us humans.

God Had Contact with His People

This practice of visitation didn't stop after Adam and Eve were expelled from the garden. Note several other examples:

Noah (Genesis 6:12–7:4)

God visited Noah regarding the evil that humanity was doing and told him about his plan to destroy the earth. God gave Noah specific instructions about how to make the ark and which animals he was to take on board along with his family members.

Abraham (Genesis 13:14–17; 15:1–16; 17:15–22)

The L ORD had said to Abram, "Leave your country, your people and your father's household and go to the land I will show you."   Genesis 12:1

God visited Abram and called him to establish a great nation, to enjoy his blessing, to make his name great, and to be a blessing to all peoples on earth. As Abram obeyed God these things came to pass. Thus began numerous visits from God.

Moses at the Burning Bush (Exodus 3:1–4:17)

In one of the most dramatic events recorded in the Bible, God confronted Moses in an isolated place as Moses was tending sheep for Jethro, his father-in-law. This passage describes how God and Moses interacted at the burning bush, where Moses was more than a little bit reluctant to be the instrument God was calling him to be.

Throughout the pre-exodus and exodus experience, Moses and God had frequent visits with each other as problems and issues arose. To see more of the dynamics, you can read the entire story in the book of Exodus. At times God took the initiative in visiting Moses; other times Moses sought God. An important relationship ingredient to note is that once Moses agreed to lead the people out of Egypt, God continued to be present as a source of encouragement and help. From this we can glean the principle that once a person agrees to do a task, the person who enlists her has a responsibility to continue to work with her as they do the job, offering additional instruction, guidance, and encouragement.

Moses at Mount Sinai (Exodus 19:3–9)

The movie The Ten Commandments dramatically portrays God's response to Moses when Moses sought him. If you've seen the movie, perhaps you recall the scene where Moses climbed to the top of Mount Sinai, which had been enveloped in a thick cloud and smoke as the ground shook and a trumpet

BE MOTIVATED: How Does the Bible Model the Importance of Visitation?

15

blast filled the air. Out of that dramatic setting God talked personally with Moses.

Part of Moses' challenge was that he was the middleman—the go-between for God and the people. Communication problems often occur when we don't deal directly with people but share messages from someone else. How valuable face-to-face visits are in helping to resolve misunderstandings and clarify issues and relationships!

Samuel (1 Samuel 3:1–14)

One of the most beautiful stories in the Bible is how God called the boy Samuel. Even though Samuel thought Eli the priest was calling him, God persisted in seeking to visit Samuel. God's personal dealings with young Samuel illustrate that age is not a significant factor when God is speaking to and leading a person.

Isaiah (Isaiah 6:1–13)

The prophet Isaiah went to the temple after the death of good King Uzziah. Not only did Isaiah have a stirring worship experience there, he also had a visit from God. Isaiah 6:1–13 describes Isaiah's worship encounter with God and also God's call for him.

When God calls someone to service, the task isn't always easy, nor is it always something he or she wants to do. God's call to Isaiah revealed that his listeners would resist and fail to respond to the message that Isaiah would speak on God's behalf.

JESUS PRACTICED VISITATION

Jesus' ministry was characterized by constant movement from place to place, as he often visited people who had needs that he chose to meet. Some of these needs were physical—various ill-nesses, blindness, paralysis, and the like—while other needs were spiritual, such as being possessed by a demon, bearing the guilt of sin, or needing a proper relationship with God. Jesus visited people in their homes as well as along the roadway. Some persons sought him out, and others he sought out. Jesus enjoyed being around people, frequenting places where both small groups and large groups gathered.

Consider these visits by Jesus:

❏ At a wedding in Cana, where he turned water into wine (John 2:1 – 10)

❏ At the home of Simon Peter, where he healed Peter's mother-in-law (Mark 1:29 – 34)

❏ At the home of Matthew, where he had dinner with this unpopular tax collector and a motley collection of his friends (Matthew 9:9 – 13)

❏ At a dinner party in the home of a Pharisee, where a woman washed his feet (Luke 7:36 – 50)

❏ At the home of Jairus the synagogue ruler, where he brought back to life the twelve-year-old daughter who had died (Mark 5:21 – 24, 35 – 43)

❏ On the road to Bethsaida, where he reached out to a blind man (Mark 8:22 – 26)

❏ At the side of a well, where he visited with an immoral Samaritan woman (John 4:7 – 26)

❏ At the home of Zacchaeus the wealthy tax collector (Luke 19:1 – 10)

❏ At the home of Martha, where he talked with Mary while Martha worked (Luke 10:38 – 42)

BE MOTIVATED: How Does the Bible Model the Importance of Visitation?

17

❏ At the village where Martha, Mary, and Lazarus lived, where he raised Lazarus from the dead (John 11:1–44)

JESUS SENT HIS DISCIPLES INTO THE HOMES OF OTHERS

Not only was Jesus himself active in visiting people, but he also instructed his disciples in the art of visitation. He gave specific instructions to the disciples as he sent them out:

"Do not go among the Gentiles or enter any town of the Samaritans. Go rather to the lost sheep of Israel. As you go, preach this message: 'The kingdom of heaven is near.' Heal the sick, raise the dead, cleanse those who have leprosy, drive out demons. Freely you have received, freely give. Do not take along any gold or silver or copper in your belts, take no bag for the journey, or extra tunic, or sandals or a staff, for the worker is worth his keep.

"Whatever town or village you enter, search for some worthy person there and stay at his house until you leave. As you enter the home, give it your greeting. If the home is deserving, let your peace rest on it; if it is not, let it return to you. If anyone will not welcome you or listen to your words, shake the dust off your feet when you leave that home or town. I tell you the truth, it will be more bearable for Sodom and Gomorrah on the day of judgment than for that town. I am sending you out like sheep among wolves. Therefore be as shrewd as snakes and as innocent as doves."   Matthew 10:5–16

When Jesus sent out the seventy-two, he added another helpful instruction. "When you enter a house, first say, 'Peace to this house.' If a man of peace is there, your peace will rest on him; if not, it will return to you" (Luke 10:5–6).

Jesus modeled for his disciples the fine art of visitation. Almost daily they saw how Jesus dealt with people in various circumstances. He took the time to teach his disciples how to visit. The disciples could multiply contacts with various individuals and minister to many more persons than Jesus could have reached by himself. Similarly, we need to be training others to engage in the ministry of visitation so that we can multiply our effectiveness. My pastor trained me in personal evangelism by taking me along and letting me observe him. Then, in time, I took the lead in presenting the gospel. How powerful the church's impact could be if more Christians would take others along and mentor them in the art of visitation and model good visitation practices!

I grew up in a small, conservative evangelical church where I was involved in such things as Bible studies, discipleship training, and missions education, as well as church visitation. We were expected not only to participate in various church activities but also to reach out through a ministry of witnessing and visitation. My growth as a Christian had roots in this setting.

I attended a denominational college and seminary. Now I seek to be a lifelong Christian learner by participating in conferences and seminars, desiring to enhance my personal skills as a disciple of Jesus Christ. But the roots for so much of what has happened throughout my life go back to that initial visitation experience in my local church.

BE MOTIVATED: How Does the Bible Model the Importance of Visitation?

19

CALLING OF THE TWELVE

As Jesus began to select the men who would be his disciples, he did so through personal invitation, visiting them face-to-face. Matthew 4:18–22 reveals how he enlisted four of these men:

> As Jesus was walking beside the Sea of Galilee, he saw two brothers, Simon called Peter and his brother Andrew. They were casting a net into the lake, for they were fishermen. "Come, follow me," Jesus said, "and I will make you fishers of men." At once they left their nets and followed him.
>
> Going on from there, he saw two other brothers, James son of Zebedee and his brother John. They were in a boat with their father Zebedee, preparing their nets. Jesus called them, and immediately they left the boat and their father and followed him.

One reason we make visits on behalf of the church is to enlist people to become leaders. As Jesus sought out those who would become his disciples, he approached each one individually, dealing with each in a personal way. When we enlist people, we should make an effort to meet with them face-to-face rather than to rely on a chance meeting in the church hallways or in the grocery store. We should be clear about what we are asking them to do, and share with them why we believe they can do the task.

THE EARLY CHURCH PRACTICED VISITATION

The story of the early Christian church is the story of how individuals shared the message of Jesus Christ in a personal way by going to people and having face-to-face encounters. Consider these examples:

- ❑ Peter visited in the home of Dorcas after she had died (Acts 9:36–43)
- ❑ Peter visited in the home of Cornelius, a Roman centurion (Acts 10:1–48)
- ❑ The apostle John spoke of visiting others (2 John 12; 3 John 13–14)
- ❑ The apostle Paul made frequent missionary journeys filled with visits with people in a variety of settings (Acts 13:1–28:31)

REWARDS OF VISITATION

I have engaged in church visitation for more than fifty years. Each time I visit I come away with a rich blessing, often in ways that surprise me. I go to try to meet a specific need, yet so often the person I'm visiting ends up brightening *my* day, leaving me with a thought or uplifting idea that boosts my spirits for days. In an unforgettable way Jesus describes the rewards of ministering to the needs of people:

> "When the Son comes in his glory, and all the angels with him, he will sit on his throne in heavenly glory. All the nations will be gathered before him, and he will separate the people one from another as a shepherd separates the sheep from the goats. He will put the sheep on his right and the goats on his left.
>
> "Then the King will say to those on his right, 'Come, you who are blessed by my Father; take your

BE MOTIVATED: How Does the Bible Model the Importance of Visitation?

21

inheritance, the kingdom prepared for you since the creation of the world. For I was hungry and you gave me something to eat, I was thirsty and you gave me something to drink, I was a stranger and you invited me in, I needed clothes and you clothed me, I was sick and you looked after me, I was in prison and you came to visit me.'

"Then the righteous will answer him, 'Lord, when did we see you hungry and feed you, or thirsty and give you something to drink? When did we see you a stranger and invite you in, or needing clothes and clothe you? When did we see you sick or in prison and go to visit you?'

"The King will reply, 'I tell you the truth, whatever you did for one of the least of these brothers of mine, you did for me.'

"Then he will say to those on his left, 'Depart from me, you who are cursed, into the eternal fire prepared for the devil and his angels. For I was hungry and you gave me nothing to eat, I was thirsty and you gave me nothing to drink, I was a stranger and you did not invite me in, I needed clothes and you did not clothe me, I was sick and in prison and you did not look after me.'

"They also will answer, 'Lord, when did we see you hungry or thirsty or a stranger or needing clothes or sick or in prison, and did not help you.'

"He will reply, 'I tell you the truth, whatever you did not do for one of the least of these, you did not do for me.'

"Then they will go away to eternal punishment, but the righteous to eternal life."   Matthew 25:31–46

THE PURPOSE OF CHURCH VISITATION

What image comes into your mind when you hear the word *visitation*? Do you picture faithful church members or pastors knocking on the doors of homes in the community, hoping to sit down and talk with people in their living rooms? This can certainly be an important part of visitation. However, such factors as the growth of sprawling suburbs, the reality of elongated working hours, a well-taught suspicion of strangers who knock on doors, the presence of glowing television screens, and the difficulty of finding people at home have all combined to make "house calls" challenging. It's reassuring to recall the insight of Jay Adams in *Shepherding God's Flock*, who links the idea of visitation with shepherding.

> The "visitation" in view in both the Old and New Testaments at its core is *oversight that shows concern for.* The concern which is at the core of biblical visitation is equivalent to a kind of remembering or *thinking about* another . . . *that leads to action. . . .*
>
> The image of knocking on doors and paying visits (as *the method* of showing concern), however, is not inherent in (or even a prominent thought related to) biblical visitation.[1]

---

[1] Jay Adams, *Shepherding God's Flock* (Grand Rapids: Zondervan, 1974), 75–76.

BE MOTIVATED: How Does the Bible Model the Importance of Visitation?

23

While it may be appropriate and advisable to visit in people's homes, there is certainly room for other methods of showing concern, such as visiting someone in the hospital, meeting someone at a coffee shop, having lunch at someone's place of employment, inviting someone to your home for a meal, and visiting with someone on the golf course or even while jogging together.

Visitation opens the way for evangelistic contacts in various creative settings, and another type of visitation has ministry and inreach as its purpose. We minister to people who already have a relationship with a local church and who have a spiritual or physical need that the church can meet. We live in a time when individuals and families face all kinds of struggles and issues in life. They too need the church's ministry through visitation in various forms. Some people know what it's like to have battled cancer or to have experienced the death of a spouse or child, which helps form a bond when ministering to people who have had similar experiences.

For example, in February 1996 I had a near-death experience from a dissecting aneurysm and had open-heart surgery. I've had the opportunity to share with several people facing similar situations in their lives. Some are believers, while others have no relationship to a church or commitment to an organized religion.

Another part of the visitation ministry within the church is to enlist people to serve in various ministries. A church never seems to have enough volunteers to carry out the ministries she is called to undertake. All too often, a few people are trying to do all or most of the church's ministry. These people experience burnout in ministry as they try to do too many tasks, and they only succeed in robbing others of an opportunity for ministry and for growth as a Christian.

The challenge and opportunities of serving in ministry need to be presented regularly. Many people do not respond to announcements from the pulpit or from methods that appeal to guilt feelings. Some church members have the gift of enlisting people to receive training and helping people find and use their spiritual gifts.

There are proper ways to enlist people for ministry and service. Whenever we ask a person to do something for God and his church, we must present the benefits for the one who is doing the ministry as well as the responsibility to meet the needs of others. As you read the following chapters, my prayer is that you would be challenged to meet needs and, even more, that you would also enlist others in the ministry of creatively connecting with people to show the concern of Jesus Christ for them, whatever their need may be.

I began this chapter by looking at how the Bible records numerous visits from God. The Bible opens with God visiting humankind; it closes with the promise of future visitations from the Lord. "Behold, I am coming soon!" A second time Jesus says, "Behold, I am coming soon!" A third time he says, "Yes, I am coming soon" (Revelation 22:7, 12, 20).

BE MOTIVATED: How Does the Bible Model the Importance of Visitation?

25

QUESTIONS FOR REFLECTION AND DISCUSSION

1. Where does church visitation fit in the hierarchy of ministries in your church? How many people participate regularly in your church's visitation ministry?

2. Select one of the examples of visitation from the Old Testament. What characteristics of these visits can help you be an effective church visitor?

3. What visitation principles can you discover from Jesus' examples of visitation? Which of these is your church engaged in at this time? Identify one you can begin to adopt and implement right now.

4. What are the advantages and disadvantages of home visitation in your church's local setting? What are some other ways of "visiting" besides making an appointment to visit in a person's home?

5. List the benefits of visitation as described in Matthew 25:31–46. Which of these rewards have you personally experienced? How did it make you feel?

TWO

Be Prepared: What Kind of Person Makes a Good Visitor?

It's Monday night at First Community Church, and five people are meeting in the church office for prayer before setting out to make visits in the community. What a rush it's been for several who hurried home from work and quickly ate a meal with the family before dashing out the door. Is this your image of what "visitation" means? Admittedly, it's the way some churches approach it—but maybe it's different in your church.

Churches approach visitation ministry in a variety of ways. Some have a church visitation/evangelism committee that has responsibility for visiting potential members of the congregation. The people whom they visit are usually those who have attended a worship service or activity and expressed interest in learning more about the church. Other churches use the small group or Sunday school ministries for visitation of potential members and members who have needs. These are typically members of the small group ministry, and they have responsibility for evangelism and outreach. Another approach is to invite church leaders (such as elders and deacons) and members to participate in the church's visitation ministry.

Each church must make her own choice as to the best way to handle her visitation needs. I approach this chapter with the conviction that every Christian has the potential to be a church visitor. I will describe some characteristics or credentials a person needs in order to be an effective visitor for the church.

Don't become discouraged if you don't possess all the characteristics, because no one person possesses them all.

POSITIVE ATTITUDE TOWARD VISITATION

Some church members don't believe that they need to invite people to church or to reach out to members who have significant needs. "After all," they contend, "people know that the church is here and they'll come if they so choose, or they'll call the church when they have needs." I've participated in church visitation for more than fifty years, some of the time as a church staff member but for the past twenty-five-plus years as a lay member. My experience as a church visitor has been positive. Granted, like many others, I face the pressure of feeling that I don't have the time to visit. But when I take the time, I always feel blessed as I meet wonderful people.

In this chapter I take the perspective of an ordinary member who has been given the awesome privilege of responding to the invitation to participate in the church's visitation ministry. A positive attitude goes a long way in preparing someone to be a good visitor.

Some people approach all of life with a positive attitude. We call them optimists. Obviously not everyone is an optimist; some see life from a negative or pessimistic point of view. As we visit in the name of Christ and his church, we must do so with a positive personal attitude. We must believe that Jesus Christ and the church can and do make a significant difference in the lives of the persons we visit.

We may be visiting a person who is an unbeliever or who engages in immoral, unethical acts. A church visitor must be real and genuine. People may exhibit a behavior or express an attitude that we cannot agree with, but we must not adopt a negative, condemnatory attitude that alienates them from the start. As Christians we should see people not as they are but as what they can become with Jesus Christ in their lives.

VISITATION HAS SPIRITUAL DIMENSIONS

As a church visitor you will be representing God in the eyes of some people. You may be the first Christian they've ever had an opportunity to speak with. Your demeanor and character may introduce someone to Jesus Christ. As you visit you have the sacred opportunity and privilege to encourage people with promises from the Bible and to pray for them. In chapter 4 I'll suggest how the use of Scripture and prayer can enhance your visitation.

We engage in a visitation ministry not in our own strength but in the strength of Jesus Christ and in the presence of the Holy Spirit. So we pray for God's guidance, asking him to help us say and do the right things. We also pray that God will prepare the hearts of the persons we visit, so that they might be receptive to our time together and to God's work in their lives.

A VISITOR'S PERSONAL CHARACTERISTICS

The list of characteristics below is not exhaustive but suggests vital qualities to help us be better visitors. At the end of the chapter there is an exercise to help assess your strengths and weaknesses as a church visitor and offer suggestions on making a weakness into a strength. These qualities are not listed in the order of their significance. While you very likely won't possess all these characteristics, some of them should be evident in your life.

Be a Spiritually Sensitive Person

Being a spiritually sensitive person does not mean that you constantly use churchy or religious language; it does mean that you pray daily and seek the guidance of the Holy Spirit in your life. You will oftentimes see God at work in your own life and in the lives of people around you. You may look at an ordinary event or activity and see beyond to the underlying spiritual truth. You help others see the hand of God in their lives. Be sure to avoid using language or terms that unchurched people would not understand. You can describe religious things, but when you do, use everyday concepts and ideas.

Be a Growing Christian

If you are to lead others into a dynamic relationship with Jesus Christ and his church, you must be a growing Christian who participates regularly in Bible study and other small group ministries. To grow means that you read your Bible and pray daily, faithfully attend worship services, and support the work of your church by your presence, influence, and finances. While you may have been involved in the church and her activities for a long time, you continue to experience the inner working of Jesus and the Holy Spirit in your life.

I'm conscious of this need in my own life. I've been involved in college and seminary education as a student and teacher for forty-plus years. Each term I continue to learn new things, which I discover through reading, interviews, and interaction with my students.

Be a Listener

Listening is a significant skill to cultivate as you visit. Too often we may think we are listening when in reality we are thinking about what we will say next. We may feel awkward with silence, particularly long periods of silence. Someone once described this as "creative silence." I feel uncomfortable with long periods of silence, but I've learned that God uses these times to speak to me or to teach me some great truth I need to know. We should listen with our whole being—our ears, our eyes, our emotions, and our bodies—giving the other person our undivided attention.

By listening we are saying to other people that they are important to us, that we value them as persons and value what they are saying. Various techniques have been developed to enhance listening. Maybe you'll find it helpful to respond to another person's comments by saying, "This is what I heard you saying." Be careful, though, not to concentrate so much on the technique that you don't hear what the person is saying. The ability to listen to others is a valuable tool for the church visitor.

Be Accepting

The people we visit have not necessarily had the same experiences or influences on their lives that we've had. I grew up in a Christian family that was active in the church. We lived in the Bible Belt, where a large percentage of people were Christians and went to church. Today many people do not have any religious background or training. The only time they've heard the name of God or Jesus has been in profanity. They have virtually no clue what the Bible is all about. Sometimes their language and behavior may offend us.

As we try to establish a relationship with the person we visit, we must affirm the person, even though we may not accept his or her lifestyle or behavior. Our task is to introduce them to Jesus and his way for their lives. *God* changes lives, not us. We can only be used by God as we see people as made in God's image and capable of an intimate, personal relationship with Jesus Christ.

Be Patient

As a church visitor we go in the presence and power of Jesus Christ; therefore we are responsible for sharing the gospel as attractively as possible. We are God's instruments, so it is God who works in the hearts and lives of people in his own time. We must take whatever time is necessary for a person to make his or her own decision. While something may be perfectly clear to us, the person we visit may not be familiar with or understand the concept. We should avoid using "churchy" language or theological terms. As we visit with people we must learn to listen to what they are saying or feeling and not try to force them to make decisions they're lukewarm about or aren't yet ready to make.

Sometimes a person accepts Jesus the first time he or she hears the message about him. Other people take some cultivating and tend to make decisions in small increments. By being patient with people we show them how God has dealt and continues to deal with us and how he will relate to them.

Be Tactful

As a church visitor you are going in the name of Jesus Christ and your church. You are trying to build a relationship with the person visited. Treat him or her as you would a new friend; approach the person in a way that shows you want to have a lifelong relationship with him or her. Sometimes people try to force us to deal with controversial topics that would sidetrack us from the real purpose of our visit—which is to share Christ or to encourage the person to become involved in the life and work of the church. I always want to keep the door open so that I can make another visit.

Be Courageous

If it's the first time you are visiting a particular person, you'll know very little about him or her, except the information the church has given you—name, address, and other factual data. Remember that you are doing God's work, so you are going in his strength and wisdom. A common reason people give for not witnessing to an unsaved person is the fear of rejection or ridicule. We must be bold in our witnessing. We go, believing that God wants us to go. The first time I visit someone I wonder how he or she will receive me—accepting me, or rejecting me. I also wonder how I will feel about him or her. Will I like him? Will I be comfortable with her? My ego is involved. No one wants to be rejected by someone else.

When Jerusalem was threatened by Sennacherib, king of the enemy nation of Assyria, the Israelites were encouraged by these words: "Be strong and courageous. Do not be afraid or discouraged because of the king of Assyria and the vast army with him, for there is a greater power with us than with him" (2 Chronicles 32:7). Likewise, as God's people we can take heart, even under difficult circumstances, knowing that God is with us.

Be Persistent

God works in his own time, not ours. Everyone has a reachable, teachable moment. There is a time in a person's life when he or she is ready to receive Jesus Christ. We do not know when that time is, or what the life needs of the person may be, so we keep going as long as God continues to lead us to do so. Have you heard the story of how a Sunday school teacher week after week visited a young man in the back of a shoe store? The teacher lost count of the number of times he had visited this man. He felt called by God to continue to visit him. Then one day the young man prayed to receive Jesus Christ into his life. God used persistence and faithful witnessing. We should be persistent in visiting others as long as God directs us to. We do not know the time of God's working to turn someone toward him.

Be Friendly

Your openness and friendliness will go a long way in encouraging people to become a part of the life of the church. Many people are lonely, even in the midst of crowds of people. They may be new to your community, or experiencing the grief of leaving a place where they were known and where they knew many people. As you visit, learn the person's name and something about his or her background. You may be his or her door into the church. Be genuine. You can invite the person to visit a worship service or a small group meeting. Since he or she will be your guest, arrange a time and place where you will meet— or better yet, offer a ride to church. Remember, you know many people at church, but you may be the only person he or she knows.

One of my teachers taught me to love people, not by telling me to do so, but by the things he said and did that showed how much he loved people. I wanted to be like him. You can't fake being friendly; you must genuinely like people and care for them. You can't make others happy, but you can help them see that you care and want to be their friend.

Be Sympathetic and Empathetic

As Jesus encountered people, he showed both sympathy and empathy toward them. He had the ability to feel what people felt. He was not afraid to show his emotions. When he learned about the death of his friend Lazarus, he wept (John 11:35). When he looked out over the city of Jerusalem, his heart was broken (Luke 19:41). One day, after Jesus had taught all day, he realized that his listeners were hungry, so he performed the miracle of feeding the five thousand (Matthew 14:13–21).

As we visit we must show people that we genuinely care for them. One way to gauge this is by how well we listen to the stories they tell us. When we have sympathy for another person, we are saying that we know or can identify with what they have felt and what has happened to them. Empathy suggests that we feel what the other person has felt. It is probably impossible to completely empathize with another, because we haven't had the same relationships or experiences. I have sympathy—and maybe even empathy—for a person who has had open-heart surgery, because I've gone through it twice. While I can sympathize with them, I also have some idea of what they're going through. Keep in mind, though, that everyone's experience is different.

Keep Confidences

You should not have to tell someone that you keep confidences. You communicate it by not sharing secrets or confidential information you've heard from or about someone else. Most church visits do not deal with issues that others would know about. As you build deeper friendships, people might share some hidden, unknown things about themselves. Thank them for sharing with you, assure them that you will pray for them, and ask if there's anything you can do to help them. You might want to pray for them right then and there. Look for something tangible and concrete to do that would be appropriate to their particular need.

Strive for a Pleasing Personal Appearance

Wear clothing that helps you feel comfortable. If you are going to do a lot of walking, wear comfortable shoes. Try not to dress either too formally or too casually—either of which can make people uncomfortable. Where and when you visit the person may determine what is appropriate clothing. Sometimes regional differences help determine appropriate dress. Also the age of the person being visited has a bearing. When I served a country church and visited during the week, casual clothes were appropriate. Think about the person you're about to visit—you want to help them feel at ease.

Someone once said, "You only have one opportunity to make a first impression." It's important how you look the first time you meet the person—maybe even as important as what you will say.

Maintain a Pleasant Personality

Although you can't totally overhaul your personality, you can be conscious of how you appear to others and how you come across. Making visits on behalf of the church is not a time to be sarcastic or to use inappropriate humor. Humor should never be used to demean another person or to make someone look bad. Yet good humor can be a wonderful way to build good relationships. Being able to laugh at one's self is a great gift.

How the person being visited perceives you is important. Do they see you as open and responsive to them? Are you the kind of person they can identify with? Do they feel comfortable with you? Many of us are not immediately transparent, and we may not reveal significant things about ourselves the first time we meet someone. Achieving a level of comfort takes time.

Make Adequate Preparations

What we do prior to making the visit is as important as the visit itself. How we prepare for the visit may well determine what happens on the visit itself. Here are some suggestions that you may find helpful:

Pray for Yourself and the Person to be Visited

I start by praying for myself—that I might have the proper spirit and that I will be sensitive to God's leadership and direction as I visit. I pray that I will listen with my ears but also with my heart. I also pray that God will remove any sin in my life that would hinder the visit. I pray for a humble spirit that will leave the results up to God, because I am his messenger and instrument. I pray that God will guide me throughout the visit, that I will know when to ask for a decision to become a follower of Jesus and when I should wait. This is *God's* work, and I must seek to do his will.

Before my visit, I pray that God will prepare the person or persons I am about to visit. I pray that he will make these people responsive to me as a person, that they will receive the message I am led to bring. If the person is unsaved, I pray that God will lead him or her to accept the salvation God offers through Jesus Christ. Sometimes the person accepts Jesus on the initial visit; sometimes he or she gives me permission to come back and share more. Other times he or she is willing to attend a worship service or a small group ministry. I have learned to accept whatever commitment the person gives.

Be Knowledgeable about the Person Visited

What do I know about the person I will visit? The data given by the church is often minimal at best—name and address, sometimes a few other brief items. Additional information and data can only be gained as I visit with the person or family. As I discover more about them, I want to report this information to the church so that other visitors can benefit from my visit. These are some questions I try to answer:

❑ How long have they lived in the community?
❑ Where did they live before moving to our community?
❑ How many people are in the family? What is the spouse's name? What are the children's names? What are their ages? Are they in school? What schools do they attend?
❑ Where do they work?
❑ What is their spiritual condition? Are they Christians? Do they belong to a church? Is this church similar to our church? How active have they been in a church?

Be Knowledgeable about Your Church

Be familiar with your church's history and background. Some churches have an information packet for people to give to those who are visited. Familiarize yourself with its contents. Be prepared to tell those you visit about your pastor and staff members—something about their background, how long they've been at the church, and any special skills or interests they have.

Find out the interests and passions of the people you are visiting. Share with them some details about particular ministries. Many churches have an area (or areas) of ministry in which they particularly excel—it may be preschoolers, children, youth, single adults, senior adults, family life, music, and so forth. Describe the potential for small group ministry in your church. The small group is where persons get to know others more intimately.

Be acquainted with your church's organization or structure—whether you have elders and deacons, or work through teams or committees. If your church has a statement of faith that describes her doctrinal beliefs, it can help to share this with those you visit. Be careful, though, in an initial visit not to give non-Christians literature filled with vocabulary and terms that may leave them confused.

You might also want to be familiar with your church's constitution and bylaws. I know of one church that has every prospective member read the doctrinal statement and also the constitution and bylaws. Doing so allows the person to understand what the church believes and how the church functions. Be sure to be sensitive as to when you provide this material. Mature Christians who are transferring from another church might find this helpful. People who have not yet professed their faith in Jesus might find it confusing.

Be Knowledgeable about Your Community and Other Churches in Your Community

Think about your feelings when you first moved to your community. What information and data would have been helpful for your adjustment during the early days of living there? Seven and a half years ago my wife and I moved to a small town thirty miles from where we had lived for seventeen years. We had often visited friends there, but we didn't know how the town was laid out, where the grocery stores were located, or where we could find the banks, medical facilities, and other important sites.

A faithful visitor shared why she did visitation for her church. When she and her family moved to a new community, an older man rang the doorbell as soon as the moving van departed. She was greeted by the words, "Welcome to our community. I've lived here a long time, and I like it here very much. I baked a plate of brownies for you and your family. I hope you enjoy them. I go to the church down the street. I hope you'll visit our church soon." She told him that they attended a church of a different denomination. His reply was, "Wonderful! Let me tell you where they're located. There are some very fine churches in this community. You're certainly welcome to visit our church for special activities we have going on every once in a while."

Get to know the evangelical churches of various denominations that are in your community. Be affirming toward and positive about them and their ministry.

What Kind of Visitor Are You?

Use the following rating scale to assess your strengths and weaknesses as a church visitor. If you are studying this book with others, you might ask another group member or a trusted friend to rate you.

Write in the blank space any number on a scale of 1 to 5 to indicate how you rate yourself (1 = you feel you are weak; 5 = this is a strength). Be honest in your responses. Don't be too critical with regard to your weaknesses or too generous with regard to your strengths

_____ Positive Attitude toward Visitation

_____ A Spiritually Sensitive Person

_____ A Growing Christian

_____ A Listener

_____ Accepting of Others

_____ Patient

_____ Tactful

_____ Courageous

_____ Persistent

_____ Friendly

_____ Sympathetic

_____ Empathetic

_____ Keeps Confidences

_____ Pleasing Personal Appearance

_____ Pleasant Personality

Review your scores. Which items had 4s or 5s? Which received 1s or 2s? (A rating of 3 indicates that you feel comfortable about this characteristic but could improve.)

Leave the Results to God

Remember that you are God's instrument as a church visitor. Present the gospel and your church in the best way possible. Whether you are trying to help a person to commit his or her life to Jesus Christ for the first time or to become a part of your church, it is a spiritual decision. The person can only respond as God's Spirit leads him or her. You may not see any reason why he or she cannot make this decision, but remember, it's *their* decision, not yours. Assure them of your continued interest and desire to be of help. Some people want more time. If so, encourage them to take whatever time they need and assure them that you'll continue to support them. Offer to answer any additional questions. Maybe you can make an appointment for a follow-up visit.

A TRAINING OPPORTUNITY

A person does not necessarily have to complete a six-week training activity in order to qualify as a church visitor. A minister or layperson responsible for church visitation could do a one-hour training session for people who are first-time visitors. She could do a couple of simulated visits, one titled "How Not to Visit." This could be quite humorous, overplaying the mistakes people make. After the role-play, let the participants identify what was done poorly and what should be avoided. The other simulation would be titled "How to Make a Good Visit."

This chapter began by describing what happens in many churches: people gather at church, get their visitation assignments, pray, and then go out to call on people. Some churches use this gathering time as a way to provide additional training in the fine art of church visitation. It need only take about five or ten minutes. The purpose is to help each person become a better church visitor.

QUESTIONS FOR REFLECTION AND DISCUSSION

1. Select one of the characteristics or qualities of a church visitor. If you already have this quality, describe how you are using it as a church visitor. If you do not have this quality, what can you do to develop it in your life?

2. Describe one of your most difficult experiences in visitation. What made it difficult? If you could replay this visit, what might you do differently?

3. Describe one of your most rewarding visits. What made it rewarding?

4. What are some rewards of being involved in visitation—both evangelistic visits and visits to help needy church members?

5. List some things you and other church leaders can do to encourage more people to carry out visits on behalf of your church.

THREE

Be Informed: What Kinds of Visits Are Possible?

Several years ago I was hospitalized for surgery. I remember being surprised when J. K. Lathem, a church member with a hearing impairment, walked into my hospital room. He knew that I didn't know sign language—what's more, I couldn't speak at the time, so he wouldn't have been able to read my lips. And yet he came because he cared about me and was concerned. He brought with him several current sports magazines he thought I would like to read. Other visitors came during my brief hospital stay, but his visit was the most meaningful. Perhaps you've been on the receiving end of "visits" as well.

That word *visit* can be used in a variety of ways—for example, to describe going to a store or going to see a doctor or a friend. But in this chapter I'll use the word to refer specifically to church visitation—going to someone to help meet a specific need, wherever he or she might be located.

In order to be clear about the term, let's further define it. Luther Rice Seminary founder Robert G. Witty states, "To visit is to minister in person."[2] Ronald Brown suggests that visitation refers to "the act of visiting or calling upon someone as an act of friendship or courtesy, or for some particular purpose."[3]

---

[2]Robert G. Witty, *Church Visitation: Theory and Practice* (Nashville: Broadman, 1967), 13.

[3]Ronald K. Brown, "A Definition of Personal Visitation," in *Going . . . One on One: A Comprehensive Guide for Making Personal Visits,* comp. Harry M. Piland (Nashville: Convention Press, 1994), 21.

When we talk about visitation in the church, we mean *personal* visitation—going person to person. Here's how Witty further defines Christian visitation: "Visitation is a Christian service whereby Christians go or come to other persons in order to understand their needs and assist them with the adequate help found only in Christ."[4] Brown further defines it as "a direct encounter by an individual with another person for the purpose of understanding and addressing the person's needs, offering encouragement and assistance in the name of Jesus, and declaring through word and/or deed the abiding love and care of God."[5] I personally like this last definition. We should be motivated to visit by a desire to show others the love of God as revealed in Jesus Christ.

I will describe in this chapter (and the next) a wide variety of visitation opportunities, but space doesn't permit me to describe all of them. Usually visitation means making a call at someone's home, a hospital, a funeral home, or a place of business. However, effectively reaching people for Jesus Christ in today's world requires using all available means and approaches to sharing his love. In addition to meeting people face-to-face, we may telephone, send a fax or an e-mail message, or write a note.

Not only can we visit in homes, but we should also be alert to opportunities to meet in restaurants, sports centers, clubs, workplaces, schools, coffee bars, and parks—or on buses, subways, ferries, and in car pools. The location possibilities are endless, as are the times. Visitation might occur at the beginning or end of a work shift, during break time, or over breakfast, lunch,

[4] Witty, *Church Visitation*, 15.
[5] Brown, "A Definition of Personal Visitation," 21.

or dinner. Obviously the timing should be at the other person's convenience. We must be flexible. Whatever creative time or place we meet, the most important consideration is that we visit *in the name of Jesus*, with openness to his leading.

Consider this example of witnessing at a creative time and place: I know a pastor who belonged to a local tennis club. A good tennis player, he often went to the club at 8:00 or 9:00 P.M. and usually found someone to play. If the person wasn't a Christian, this pastor would get him to agree that if the pastor won, this person would come to his church to hear him preach. The pastor usually won—and a number of men heard him preach and became believers in Jesus as a result.

VISITATION GUIDELINES

Before describing types of visits, let me suggest some applicable guidelines for any type of visit. Church visitation requires that those who visit are spiritually fit. We need to check our relationships with family members, friends, and work associates. Our participation and involvement in the services, activities, and ministries should model what we are inviting others to join. In other words, we must examine our own lives to see if there is anything that could be a barrier to others. Consider these guidelines:

Pray

How easy it is to forget the critical role that prayer preparation plays! We offer ourselves to God, asking that he would use us as his instruments during the visit. We prepare ourselves by praying that God would remove any hidden sin. We ask

God to go before us and prepare each person we visit to be receptive. We pray for the Holy Spirit's leadership and guidance in what to say and how to approach each person.

Team Up with a Visitation Partner

Go with another person, particularly if you are visiting a person of the other gender. Having a visitation partner can be an encouragement, because we have an ally in prayer who shares our desire to see the person receive a blessing.

Be sure to identify yourself. People are justifiably cautious about letting strangers into their home. If the visit is to take place in a home, I might make a phone call in advance. If I haven't done so, I might say, when the door is opened, "Hello, I'm Jerry Stubblefield from Hopewell Church, and this is Charles Smith. Your name was given to us by.... We'd like to talk briefly with you about our church. May we come in?"

Always be prepared. Have an appropriate Scripture to share with the person. I always carry with me a small Bible that fits easily into my pocket. Have appropriate literature to hand out should the need or opportunity arise.

TWO TYPES OF VISITS

Inreach/Ministry

The focus of inreach/ministry visitation is involvement with people who are already under the church's umbrella (but they may no longer be actively attending worship services or participating in programs and activities). These are church members on the fringes whose names are on the church roll but who are not visible when the church gathers. In major denominations, between 20 and 30 percent of total membership is inactive. The church needs to show concern for such members.

Still others are active, participating members of the church who have a physical, emotional, or spiritual need that the church can and should meet. Members of a Bible study group or another small group may be especially well positioned to minister to them. These ministry visits will be described in greater detail in chapter 4.

Outreach/Evangelism

The focus of outreach/evangelism visitation is to minister and witness to those who are not a part of your church or who are unbelievers. You might witness to someone who attends your church and participates in its activities but has never accepted Jesus Christ as their personal Savior. Many churches could reap a rich harvest of lost souls by focusing on people (and their families) already involved in the church. By witnessing to them and encouraging them, you may be instrumental in the most important decision of their lives—accepting Jesus Christ.

A large percentage of adults in America are either unsaved or not members of a church in the community in which they now live. The numbers range from 60 percent to more than 80 percent, depending on the part of the country. However, this does not mean that all our outreach/evangelism efforts must be limited to personal witnessing. Ministering to a person's needs may provide the opportunity for sharing one's faith in the hope that this person will accept Jesus Christ as Savior and Lord.

Another group of people who visit our churches are those who are believers but do not belong to a local church. Some might be new to our community. We visit them to encourage them to be active in their faith by becoming members of our church. A vital church will have a keen interest in reaching Christians who are not members of any local congregation.

Visiting the Unchurched

In past generations when Christians moved to a new community they immediately sought out a church and joined in a few weeks. It was the popular thing to do. The current pattern for many people is to "church-shop." They begin by attending a worship service. If they have preschoolers, they check out the church nursery to be sure that the church has a clean, attractive, and well-staffed place. If they have school-age children or youth, they are interested in Sunday school or Bible study for them. They want to know what activities or programs a church has.

There are multiple ways a church can minister to unchurched persons. A church some distance from a university has a church bus that transports students to the morning worship service. They invite them to stay for lunch (a hot meal — including homemade pies) and Bible study after worship. The church captures numerous opportunities to minister to these students, who attend the church in large numbers, even though it is not located close to the campus.

Two women leaders from a coed Bible study group in a church I served were constantly making contact with people who had moved into town. They invited women to one of their homes for coffee and frequently hosted three or four couples for a meal. As a result many young couples joined the church because of the kindness of these two women.

I recall having visited many families who moved to our community and visited our church. One couple began attending Bible study and the morning worship service. They had been leaders in a church that had disbanded. As we visited I told them about our church. They had some questions that were easily answered. They really enjoyed the Bible study class but wanted to know how they could get a name tag—like other class members had. I assured them that name tags could be arranged. I talked to the Bible study leader and shared their concern, and he responded, "We can take care of that!" The very next Sunday the couple arrived for Bible study, and their name tags were waiting. A few weeks later they joined the church. People who are new to a church need to feel that they belong, that they are like others. Personal name tags made this couple feel a part of the Bible study fellowship. They became faithful members and gifted leaders.

Following Up with People Who Visit Your Church

Most churches regularly have visitors at their worship services. Their presence indicates an interest in your church—and the potential that someone will become a Christian and a church member. It is helpful if you get names, addresses, telephone numbers, ages, church relationships, and the like. There are different ways to do this—through information gathered by greeters at an information booth, or by signing a guest book, a visitors' card, or a registration pad. (Bear in mind that some may not fill out an information card or sign a registration pad, even though they come back week after week.)

People contacted within seventy-two hours of a church visit have a high potential of eventually becoming members. There are many different patterns of following up on visitors:

❏ One church's pastor calls visitors on Sunday afternoon to express his pleasure at their visit. He lets them know that someone from the church will contact them soon. Then on Monday morning he gives the information to a secretary, who records the data on an information card assigned either to a staff member or church leader. The visitor is visited as soon as possible, and a report is given to the pastor.

❏ Another church assigns someone to collect visitors' cards from the offering plate and distribute them at the end of the service to church leaders, who either call or visit the home within forty-eight hours.

❏ In other churches either the pastor or a staff member contacts each visitor as soon as possible. The information they obtain is noted on a card, and those who attend Wednesday evening prayer service are asked to take a card, contact a person, and report to the church the results.

Any active church member should be able to contact people who visit the church. It is usually best if two members (often either a married couple or two persons of the same gender) make the visit together. The team should decide who will take the lead (the other will fill a prayerful supportive role while the visit is made). Your purpose is to tell people how pleased you are that they attended a service or activity. Once you discover needs and interests the church can meet, you'll want to share additional information about the church and her ministries.

Visiting Other Prospective Members

In addition to lists of potential members who attended a church service or activity, other names can come from community door-to-door surveys, telephone calling, or church members who supply the names of friends they think might be interested.

Most prospects need cultivating, so the visitor starts by looking for ways to extend warm friendship. Often several follow-up visits will be made to the same person. Those who cultivate prospects should

❏ magnify friendship.
❏ follow the leadership of the Holy Spirit.
❏ listen attentively.
❏ focus on the other person's interests.
❏ build on previous contacts.
❏ follow up with acts of kindness.
❏ recognize a birthday and other special events.
❏ take something to leave with the person.
❏ be patient.
❏ pray for the person.
❏ keep the visit brief.

Visiting People Who Are Nonbelievers

People use various methods to share their faith and help others become Christians. Salvation comes from God through his Son, Jesus Christ—not through a particular method. Some people approach witnessing as though they were selling a product and are willing to do almost anything to get the person to accept what they are offering. As you witness be sure that you understand the Bible and can locate Scripture passages quickly. A popular approach is to use the "Roman Road" (selected verses from the book of Romans), where you lead a person through the following verses:

- ❏ Romans 1:18   Power for Salvation
- ❏ Romans 3:23   All Have Sinned
- ❏ Romans 6:23   Penalty of Sin
- ❏ Romans 5:8   God's Great Grace
- ❏ Romans 2:4   Repentance
- ❏ Romans 10:9   Confession
- ❏ Romans 10:13   Acceptance

As you share with the person, do not quote the Bible passages, but read from your Bible or use a copy the other person may have. Take enough time to ensure that he or she understands. (You might ask them to put it into their own words.)

The person may not respond positively the first time he or she hears the gospel presentation. Keep the door open to make a return visit. Set a time when you will return to answer any questions or concerns or to follow up on a decision to accept Jesus as Savior.

In addition to the Roman Road approach, there are many other methods available—or you can work out your own presentation. Gideon Bibles have a "way of salvation" listed in the front of each Bible or Scripture portion. As a youth I used a *Christian Worker's New Testament* that had a series of underlined Bible verses one could use. You should use an approach with which you are familiar or comfortable.

Some witnessing programs encourage you to memorize your testimony—what you will say in presenting the gospel. If you use this approach, put the story of your experience of coming to faith in Jesus Christ in your own words, and share it as you would normally talk. (You may want to prepare versions that have different themes, so you can give your testimony a second, third, or fourth time as needed to the same person.)

Remember that your primary purpose is to point someone to a relationship with Jesus Christ. Our concern is more about a person's salvation than about whether he or she joins our church. Never forget, however, that each new believer needs to be involved in discipleship. Evangelism without discipleship is faulty evangelism. New believers should be invited to be involved in a small group experience or one-on-one relationship soon after their conversion experience. Who better to encourage the discipleship process than the one God used to lead a person to salvation—to help this person make a good beginning in the Christian life?

The reality is, unless people get involved in a small group or cultivate a close one-on-one friendship, they are likely to disappear within a few months. Utilize discipleship materials for new believers. A new believer needs the support and encouragement of other believers.

In this chapter I've discussed the critical role of visitation in evangelism. But it's not the only way church members can participate in visitation. In the next chapter I'll explore other creative ways to reach out to needy people.

QUESTIONS FOR REFLECTION AND DISCUSSION

1. What are the two major types of church visits that take place in the church today?

2. What ideas did you glean from this chapter about following up with people who visit your church?

3. How would you explain the gospel if you were visiting a receptive person who had not yet become a Christian? What Scripture verses would you use?

4. What kinds of contacts are your members making with persons who are unchurched? Talk about ways to improve both the quantity and quality of visitation contacts with unchurched persons in your community.

FOUR

Be Involved: What Kinds of Inreach Visits Can Be Made?

Many people have come to equate *visitation* with home visits for the purpose of evangelizing persons who do not believe in Jesus Christ. But this purpose is only part of what's involved in visitation. In this chapter I'd like us to expand our horizons and consider some ways church members can participate in what I call "inreach/ministry visits" to people who are already a part of the church.

VISITING THE SICK

Most families are affected by illness at some point or other over the course of time. Whether or not hospitalization is required, we feel very vulnerable when confronted with the realization that illness can and does happen to *us*—not just to someone else. The illness can lead to short-term or long-term confinement. A visitor may encounter a need for hope in the midst of hopelessness, a need for encouragement in fighting off depression, a desire for sympathy, and a need for help in overcoming fear. As you visit try to identify Scripture passages that speak to these and other related issues. Chapter 5 will offer several suggestions.

Prior to making a home visit to a sick person, call to make sure it would be a good time to come over. Keep your visit brief. Also be aware of the needs of the caregiver. In cases of long-term illness, the caregiver often needs respite care, which a church visitor may be able to provide.

Hospital Visitation

In Matthew 25:36 Jesus says, "I was sick and you looked after me." A hospital visit is a tangible way for a Christian to say, "I care for you. I'm concerned about you." As you visit be aware of the condition of the hospitalized person. A critically ill person may be in a unit where he or she is receiving specialized care. While you may not be able to see the patient, you can visit with family members who anxiously wait for their loved one to show some improvement or for some update to come from the doctor. This is a great time to offer support and encouragement, even in the gravest of circumstances. At times like these you can share a few words in a hallway or in a lounge—or even by offering to go with them to the coffee shop.

Here are some guidelines to remember as you make a hospital visit:

❏ Visit only during posted visiting hours (check the Yellow Pages of the local telephone directory or call the hospital in advance).
❏ Keep your visit brief.
❏ Do not awaken a sleeping patient. Feel free to leave a note.
❏ Be positive and affirming.
❏ Ask if you may pray with him or her and perhaps read a couple verses of Scripture. (Sometimes there is too much noise and confusion, or too many people in the patient's room, to have a spoken prayer. You can have an opened-eye prayer where, through normal conversation, you can

share what you're asking God for on the person's behalf.)
- ❑ Keep your voice low.
- ❑ Do not inquire about his or her condition.
- ❑ Be a good listener.
- ❑ Sit where the patient can easily see you.
- ❑ Try to remember what it was like the last time you were ill.
- ❑ Remember that you are a guest in the hospital. If a nurse or doctor comes into the room while you are visiting, excuse yourself and step out into the hall or go to a waiting room until they've completed their task.

Possible Scripture verses to use during a hospital visit are

- ❑ Psalm 46; Psalm 91:1–6: passages of strength
- ❑ Romans 8:35–39; Ephesians 3:14–19: passages of encouragement
- ❑ Psalm 23:2; 2 Corinthians 1:3–4: passages of awareness of the Lord's presence

In many metropolitan areas it's time-consuming to go to several hospitals on a regular basis, especially if they're located in different areas of the city. One pastor solved this problem by selecting six retired men whom he trained to do hospital visitation. Each man took a day and visited all the church members who were hospitalized. When there was a critical need, the pastor would be informed so that he also could visit the patient or the family. This church had a saying: "You don't want to be so sick that the pastor comes to visit you!" These men provided a significant ministry and in turn were richly blessed, as were those whom they visited.

Visiting Shut-Ins

Many people are unable to leave their homes and may spend most of their time in bed, needing assistance in food preparation, bathing, or other basic chores. It can be lonely and depressing when a person can't go shopping, attend church, or visit with friends and family members. The same Scripture passages suggested above for a hospital visit would speak to the needs of shut-ins. When you cannot make a home visit, you can visit by means of telephone, card, letter, or e-mail message.

Many churches record their morning worship service and make cassette tapes that are available for shut-ins. (The church may provide a cassette player that can be left in the home.) Some visitors take a tape each week and listen to the worship service with the person they visit. If there is a caregiver in the home, you might invite him or her to listen to the service also.

Before visiting, telephone to confirm your expected time of arrival. If the person cannot open the door, agree on how you will gain entrance. If there is a caregiver in the home, offering respite care would help both the caregiver and the shut-in. You might plan to stay a bit longer and be an encouragement to the caregiver. Remember that you bring a change of pace—and that you are there only for a short time, while the caregiver is there constantly.

In some churches, two or three leaders and their spouses come and have a brief communion service periodically in the home. This can help the shut-in to remember that he or she is a vital member of the church.

Visiting the Terminally Ill

All of us will die someday—though most of us do not know when. The terminally ill person has been told that his or her life expectancy is limited. The person and family may experience any number of emotions. Before you visit a terminally ill person, it can be helpful to take some time to think about your own life: If you knew that your days were numbered, how could someone best help you? What would your needs be? What are some things you would not appreciate? Jot down some ideas. On the basis of these ideas, how can you help the person you are planning to visit? Some of the needs and concerns of a terminally ill person are

- ❏ having a friend who listens without interrupting.
- ❏ being heard without incurring someone's judgmental response.
- ❏ engaging in open, honest conversation about any subject.
- ❏ knowing that faith, hope, and love abide forever (focusing on the eternal).
- ❏ becoming reconciled with family, friends, and God.
- ❏ sensing a genuine understanding from others.
- ❏ having the freedom to ask why this happened and what can be done about it.
- ❏ knowing what to expect.
- ❏ experiencing complete forgiveness and God's intimate friendship.
- ❏ knowing that family members and loved ones will be cared for after his or her death.

William David Cooper gives this advice: "Throughout the visit be sensitive to human dignity, give emotional and spiritual support, help to resolve needs that surface, enhance relationships, facilitate hope, continue to listen attentively, and affirm the whole person."[6]

Always obtain permission to visit, whether the terminally ill person is in the hospital or at home. Be sensitive to the needs of the person and family. It may be appropriate for you to pray during the visit, but always ask permission. The person or a family member may want to pray aloud, or a silent prayer may be appropriate. Ask if you may visit again. Express thanks for the time you had together.

As in all cases when it is not possible to make a personal visit to a terminally ill patient, send cards or notes with a personal message. Telephone calls to the home or hospital room may provide encouragement to the patient and family. Assure them that you are praying for them.

Here are some Scripture verses you may wish to share as words of hope in tough times:

- Psalm 91:15
- Psalm 132:2
- Isaiah 1:6
- Mark 6:13
- Mark 11:24
- Luke 5:15
- Luke 10:34
- Luke 11:39
- Luke 22:42
- John 15:7
- James 5:14
- 1 John 2:27
- 1 John 3:22

---

[6]William David Cooper, "Making a Visit to the Terminally Ill," in *Going . . . One on One: A Comprehensive Guide for Making Personal Visits*, comp. Harry M. Piland (Nashville: Convention Press, 1994), 78–81.

Visiting in a Long-Term Care Facility

Nursing homes (often called long-term care facilities) provide various levels of medical care. The persons who live there are not patients or guests but residents. Not all the residents are old; many are young or middle-aged adults who have suffered an injury or an illness that requires more care than the family can give.

These are some of the qualities needed by those who visit persons in long-term care facilities:

❏ being a good listener
❏ being sensitive and empathetic
❏ being flexible
❏ being joyful
❏ being authentic
❏ being able to provide spiritual affirmation

Visitors may go in groups and visit several residents at the same time. One adult Bible study group in our church goes monthly. They lead a brief worship service with the singing of hymns and the sharing of a short devotional. Then they spend a few moments talking to each resident—including those who have stayed in their rooms. (Most residents do not have a private room, so be sure to acknowledge each person in a room.)

Here are some suggestions that can help your experience go well:

❏ Observe the policies of the facility, including visiting hours.
❏ Be natural, cheerful, positive, and spontaneous.

❏ Touch the person on the arm or shoulder to show that you care.

❏ Compliment the person in some way.

❏ Ask the resident's opinion about something.

❏ Be considerate of the resident's physical needs and limitations.

❏ Affirm the person's faith and pray for him or her.

❏ Be sure to do what you tell a resident you will do.

❏ Don't be afraid to show your emotions—laugh or shed tears.

❏ Be alert to opportunities to minister to the staff. A kind word goes a long way toward building rapport.

VISITING SENIOR ADULTS

We may think that the majority of senior adults reside in institutional care, but the fact is that 93 percent of people over the age of sixty-five live in their own homes or with a relative or friend. They are generally quite active and able to meet all or most of their own needs. A number of these folks have provided financial support and leadership for the church for many years. Percentagewise, they are the most faithful attendees of church services and programs.

Some senior adults have continued to work full-time or part-time. Those who have fewer daily responsibilities often are open to having visitors come to their homes. Visitors to senior adults need to be good listeners—and they may want to consider making longer visits. As I've visited senior adults, sometimes staying an hour or more and then telling them that I have to leave, they frequently say, "You don't have to be in a hurry." If you are an attentive listener, you will hear a lot about their family and events that happened when they were much younger. Sometimes it's appropriate and appreciated if you take magazines, cassettes, and videotapes to leave with them. Generally senior adults appreciate anything you do for them.

VISITING THOSE IN JAILS AND PRISONS

A church can designate specific persons who wish to visit jails on the church's behalf. These names will be given to the proper authorities, who will approve these visitors. Usually a person in a jail or detention center has either been charged with a crime but has not gone to trial or has been sentenced and is awaiting a prison stay. Some jails have visiting rooms where family members, attorneys, and other approved persons can visit. In other jails you visit inmates in a holding cell where several inmates are housed.

Generally, visits to inmates are made at the request of a family member or friend. To visit an inmate in a correctional facility, the inmate has to request a visit from you—and you will be put on an approved list.

Your choice of clothing is important when you make this visit. You must not wear anything that resembles what the inmates wear (denim, for example). Most correctional institutions have posted visiting days and hours that are strictly observed. Before entering the facility you will be asked questions about whether you are carrying any objects that are not allowed. You may also be subjected to a body search, usually done with a metal detector. Women are not permitted to carry in a purse, but they must take their driver's license for identification purposes. As a guest of the correctional facility, you must strictly abide by its rules. Failure to do so could result in your being permanently banned from future visits.

Your purpose in visiting is to offer support and encouragement to both inmates and families. Your presence shows that you care. (Not everyone is well suited to visit in this setting. Some people are claustrophobic and cannot handle being behind bars.)

Here are some do's and don'ts for a visitor to a prison:

❏ Do accept the time parameters set for visitation.
❏ Do obey without question all instructions given by any custodial officer.
❏ Do write to the inmate as often as possible (use the church's address, not your home address).
❏ Do ask the inmate about the future (help him or her deal with realistic, achievable goals).
❏ Do learn the language of the inmate (inmates have their own jargon; not understanding what they mean might cause you to jump to incorrect conclusions).
❏ Do pray, and be sure to leave the results with God.
❏ Do not take anything into or out of the jail for an inmate (no matter how convincing the inmate may be or how urgently the request is made).
❏ Do not get involved in legal matters (there are attorneys for these things).
❏ Do not inquire about the inmate's crime or other matters related to criminal activity. (As a lay visitor you are not protected under confidentiality statutes; you could be forced to testify against the inmate.)

❏ Do not visit other inmates without permission (however, you could be on more than one inmate's approved list).
❏ Do not become a victim of manipulation.
❏ Do not underestimate the value of your presence and the potential of the Holy Spirit to work in the life of an inmate (see 1 Corinthians 3:5–7).
❏ Do not be easily discouraged.[7]

VISITING THOSE WHO HAVE DISABILITIES

People who have physical, emotional, or mental disabilities need the care and attention provided by church members. An impairment should never set someone apart. We should treat *everyone* with dignity and respect. A person who has a disability is just like any other person in all aspects—needs, wants, reactions—and should never be avoided because of one particular "challenge" in his or her life. Recognize and rejoice in the many opportunities that exist for rich relationships with such persons.

Persons with Hearing Impairments

Two of my family's dearest friends had hearing impairments. We attended the same church and had children who were about the same age. Although both parents had hearing impairments, their children had normal hearing. We spent time together, particularly in those times when our children played together; we shared meals together. The couple was able to read lips and use sign language to communicate. The wife's

---

[7]For more on visiting inmates, see Bobby Cox, "Making a Visit in a Correctional Institution," in *Going . . . One on One*, 92–94.

speech was such that you could understand her; the husband sometimes mouthed the words.

Several years ago I had the privilege of directing a day camp for children with hearing impairments (ages six through seventeen). All of our camp counselors had developed the skill of signing. The few signs I learned helped me work with the children, and my experience has taught me that individuals with hearing impairments are warm, friendly people who respond in the same ways others do.

A person with a hearing impairment needs someone who can communicate either by sign language or by speaking slowly and distinctly enough to allow him or her to read your lips. Remember that their response is not impaired. They respond to hugs, smiles, and laughter.

If no one in your church knows sign language, seek out a teacher who could offer a class. If you have no one who is able to interpret the communication of someone who has a hearing impairment, recruit and train persons for this ministry. In the meantime find someone who is willing to communicate in whatever ways are possible—writing things down, for example—but don't hesitate to reach out.

Persons with Visual Impairments

You may encounter those whose eyesight is greatly limited, even with corrective lenses, as well as those who may not be able to see at all. Most persons with visual impairments have developed their other senses to a fine art. There is no reason why a visually impaired person cannot attend a regular Bible study group and worship service, as long as someone helps him or her get there.

These folks should be treated as you would treat any other person. They are intelligent, sensitive, and friendly. Do not offer help unless the person asks or gives permission for it. Your church could help them be more involved by providing Bible study materials, Bibles, and hymn books in Braille.

Persons with Physical Disabilities

Persons who have physical disabilities may walk slowly or use crutches or wheelchairs. Approach them as you would approach any other person. Greet them with a smile. Usually touching is permissible. Be very careful not to assume that persons with physical disabilities have nothing to offer. Many are intelligent and have wonderful leadership skills. Be sure that your church is equipped so that hallways are wide enough for wheelchairs and there are ramps wherever stairs are found— ideally an elevator that allows passage from one floor to another.

As Woody Parker points out, "Persons with physical impairments are more like all other persons than they are different. They seldom want our sympathy." According to Parker, your visit will be meaningful only in direct proportion to how well your church receives and supports the person with the impairment.[8]

Before your church can minister to people who have physical disabilities, you might need to evaluate your church's attitudinal openness and her accessibility. Be prepared to become an advocate for ministry to people with special needs.

---

[8]Woody Parker, "Making a Visit to a Person with a Physical Disability," in *Going . . . One on One,* 182–83.

FAMILY VISITS

Birth of a New Baby

The birth of a child is usually a joyous time for the family. You might be able to make a visit in the hospital, but these days new mothers usually don't stay for more than a day or two.

The birth of a new baby provides a wonderful time for pre-school teachers to visit in the home, especially those who work with infants. People often bring a gift for a new baby. If there are other children, bring a small gift for them also. (Everyone pays a lot of attention to the new baby; also the baby requires a lot of time from the parents, and older children may feel unloved or unimportant at this time.)

The above scenario assumes that the new baby is healthy. What if there are problems? A visit to the hospital or the home is appropriate, although you may be thinking, *I never know what to say; I don't have any pearls of great wisdom to offer.* You may simply want to say, "I just wanted to be with you." When I've carried out that kind of visit, often the person hugged me or took my hand. The ministry of presence is worth a million words. Explore ways you and other church members can help the family: taking care of other children, doing the laundry or housecleaning, preparing food for the family, providing transportation to and from the hospital, taking older children to school—doing whatever the family needs. Assure them of your continued prayers while also doing other tangible things that can greatly help the family.

I've assumed this is a family from your church, but it may be a family in your community who has no connection to your church and maybe even no relationship with the Lord. What a wonderful way to show them the love of Jesus Christ in action!

Problems with Children

When problems occur with children, parents often struggle with

❑ concern about what others may think.
❑ guilt. (Where did I fail? How did I go wrong?)
❑ feelings of helplessness.
❑ the need for accurate information.
❑ a desire for assurance.
❑ an awareness that others care.

It isn't necessary that a church visitor has had problems with his or her own children, though those experiences can help in identifying with what the family is feeling. It is important that the visitor is someone who knows the child and the parents. Ask yourself several questions:

❑ How would I feel if this happened to my son or daughter?
❑ What would I want most to hear from my friends?
❑ Where can I suggest they go for help?
❑ Am I making this visit for them, for their child, or for myself?[9]

The ministry of your presence can be a great encouragement to the child and the parents.

Death in the Family

Death comes in many ways. Death may be due to old age, disease, or an accident. Death may occur suddenly, or it may

---

[9]Wade Rowatt, "Making a Visit to Parents of a Teen in Trouble," in *Going . . . One on One*, 194.

come after a long, lingering illness. Family members feel a wide range of emotions surrounding the nature of death and how close their relationship was with the person. It's always helpful for church visitors to remember their own feelings when they lost a loved one.

Because of a childhood experience I feel uncomfortable visiting funeral homes or the homes of persons who have died. But I've learned that the greatest gift I can give a grieving family is the ministry of presence. Before I go to visit the family, I usually fret about what I can say to comfort or help. Often I'll simply say something like this: "I heard what happened, and I wanted to be with you." This often leads to a hug, and the conversation goes from there. The fact that you are there at such a time is enough. Be sensitive to all the emotions they may be experiencing—shock, anger, guilt, denial, or acceptance. These are all a natural part of the grief process. The sooner grieving persons can express these emotions, the faster they will be able to work through their grief.

Special occasions are especially difficult for the surviving family members—Christmas, birthdays, wedding anniversaries, and other important days. A visit or telephone call around these times can be very meaningful.

Marital Problems

You don't need to be a marriage counselor to visit with couples that have problems. As you visit, you do so as a Christian friend. They may or may not want to share their problems with you. Be a sympathetic listener, but do not take sides. Do not give advice, because if they do what you suggest, you become responsible for the consequences of their actions. You could point out various options, but they must choose the actions they will take. You might want to suggest they see a professional counselor or a member of the church's pastoral staff. Through it all you can continue to be a supportive friend.

Loss of a Job

Being unemployed was once typically a "blue-collar worker problem," not a "white-collar worker problem"—but now it can affect anyone. Imagine how you would feel if you lost your job: shock, grief, anxiety, isolation, loneliness, fear of failure, frustration, anger, sadness, depression, and more.

Most churches have members who own companies that may be able to employ those without jobs. You might organize a list of people who offer employment possibilities, and then post the list on a bulletin board. Persons who are looking for a job might benefit from help in writing a résumé or preparing for an interview. Some experienced person in the church could undoubtedly assist them. A person who has lost a job might appreciate receiving an invitation to get together for breakfast or lunch, where you have a great opportunity to show concern and to allow him or her an occasion to talk.

VISITS ON BEHALF OF THE CHURCH

Visits to Offer Encouragement

The purpose of an encouragement visit is for a Christian to attempt to alleviate the hurt and pain in someone's life. This visit may be planned, or it may take place as you meet someone when you're out and about. It can be a home visit or a casual encounter in a store—or the visitor may use the telephone or send an e-mail message or a fax. It is typically best to minister to the person face-to-face. High touch can be appreciated in an era of high tech. Everyone needs encouragement from time to time and in different stages of life—particularly at various crisis points in the life cycle, such as illness, grief over relocating to another community, divorce, broken relationships, children going away to college, caring for aging parents, and the like.

The one who makes an encouragement visit must be a person who is sensitive to the feelings and needs of others. The first step of encouragement is to acknowledge the pain the other person is feeling.

Here are some do's and don'ts for making visits that offer encouragement:

❏ Do realize that people who are vulnerable with you pay you a great compliment.
❏ Do be worthy of people's trust.
❏ Do listen with your ears, eyes, and heart.
❏ Do recognize warning signs.
❏ Do communicate hope.
❏ Don't tell people you know just how they feel.
❏ Don't try to have all the answers.
❏ Don't let others become dependent on you.
❏ Don't think you have to defend God.[10]

Visits to the Newly Divorced

No church would ignore the death of one of her members. Yet when a person goes through a divorce, the church often acts

---

[10]James E. Taulman, "Making a Visit to Offer Encouragement," in *Going . . . One on One,* 129–31.

as though nothing unusual has happened. Divorce creates in a divorced man or woman the same kinds of emotions as death, because divorce represents the death of a relationship. Newly divorced persons experience such emotions as shock, anxiety, anger, guilt, grief, paranoia, and more.

The visit's purpose is to offer support and encouragement to divorced persons. Some churches offer divorce recovery workshops and have people who are trained to help deal with emotions and pain during this time.

Divorced persons need to establish new friendships and relationships, because many of their past relationships were couple-oriented. Offering friendship is usually welcomed, as long as you don't come on too strong.

Both men and women who are newly divorced have needs that church people can and should meet. Some may need help with household chores, because their former spouse had the responsibility for those. Children of divorced persons need relationships with adults other than their parents.

Visits to Nurture a New Believer

It's important for a new believer to begin a discipleship process as soon as possible. One church developed an "Encourager Program for New Believers." This church trained people from various small Bible study groups to follow up with new believers. Church members visited soon after a person's decision to believe in Jesus was made and brought a discipleship manual to work through. The new believer and the encourager together attended Bible study and worship, went out on the outreach/evangelism visitation program, and reviewed the discipleship manual. Over the course of thirteen weeks the new believer was discipled and became involved with a small group. This church lost very few new believers through the back door.

Visits to Show Care for Absentees

With today's computer software—and potentially better record-keeping capabilities—a church should be well equipped to keep up with her members and their activity. Whether a person is absent from worship or a Bible study group, the problem goes beyond their absence to the reason for it—personal illness, family needs, some misunderstanding, or a multitude of other circumstances. By faithfully tracking members and prospects, the church stays aware of people's needs, and outreach/evangelism leaders can be poised to meet such needs.

The church visitor goes in a spirit of concern and caring. You care about the person and about what is happening. Your sole motivation is to provide any help you can. You go in the spirit of Jesus Christ—not to condemn, criticize, or belittle the person.

Chronic absenteeism can often be avoided by taking a preventive measure such as proficient follow-up the first time or two a person is absent. Unless checked, a chronic absentee eventually becomes a dropout to a Bible study group and to church involvement. As R. Wayne Jones states, "Dropout begins with one absence for which there is no follow-up ministry."[11]

Visits to Reclaim Inactive Members

An inactive church member, according to Neil E. Jackson Jr., is "a person who has not attended any services of the church in

---

[11]R. Wayne Jones, "Making a Visit to a Chronic Absentee," in *Going . . . One on One*, 104.

at least six months."[12] This may describe many church members who attend only on Easter and Christmas.

Those making these visits should be positive and possess a good knowledge of the Bible. They should possess a compassionate and understanding spirit and a willingness to listen. During these visits the visitor might have an opportunity to review what it means to be a Christian; thus he or she should know how to lead a person to make a profession of faith. Church members who have become inactive need loving Christian care. The visitor should anticipate making more than one visit.

Before making the initial contact, it is wise to telephone ahead, tell the person who you are, and agree on a time for your visit. In this phone call you may discover vital information— maybe even the reason they are not attending. They may be attending—or have joined—another church, or you may find out that the person has moved out of the community or may even be deceased

During your first visit you seek to gather information. Try to answer any questions. Neil Jackson suggests some do's and don'ts for the first visit:

❏ Do be on time.
❏ Do listen to the person.
❏ Do ask questions to discover reasons why the person is not attending.
❏ Do offer suggestions that may satisfy the person's needs.

---

[12]Neil E. Jackson Jr., "Making a Visit to Reclaim an Inactive Church Member," in Going . . . One on One, 106.

❏ Do accept responsibility for part of the problem they may be having.
❏ Do encourage the person to suggest improvements.
❏ Do offer alternatives for involving inactive members.
❏ Do inquire about other needs.
❏ Do share information about upcoming special church events.
❏ Do talk about the value of attending a small Bible study group.
❏ Do speak positively about the worship services.
❏ Do be gentle and soft-spoken.
❏ Do keep your visit brief (fifteen to thirty minutes).
❏ Do arrange for a return visit.
❏ Do write a follow-up note of appreciation.
❏ Don't heap guilt on the inactive church member.
❏ Don't argue.
❏ Don't pretend to have all the answers.[13]

Here are some Scripture verses that encourage worship and fellowship:

❏ Psalm 119:11
❏ Luke 14:23
❏ 2 Timothy 2:15
❏ Hebrews 10:25
❏ 2 Peter 3:18

---

[13]See Jackson, "Making a Visit to Reclaim an Inactive Church Member," 109.

Elder and Deacon Family Ministry Visits

Some churches use their elders and deacons to minister to families. Each elder/deacon team may be assigned eight to ten family units, whom they visit at regular intervals.

A portion of the elder/deacon meetings is spent sharing about the families—being careful, of course, not to break confidences. The group prays for these families and their special needs. This is a wonderful way to expand the church's ministry beyond what the pastoral staff can do. Pastors will also visit, but the primary ministry comes from the elder/deacon team.

In this chapter I've described just some of the ways in which church members can be involved in the area of visiting and caring for needs of people who are part of the church. I have not intended this to be an exhaustive listing. Rather, I hope to open your eyes to the wide range of opportunities that exist. Are you sensing specific ways the Lord wants you to be involved in this high and special calling?

QUESTIONS FOR REFLECTION AND DISCUSSION

1. What kinds of visits does your church excel in making? Who are the people that make these visits significant? What makes these visits special?

2. Identify ways your church can discover the needs of people in your community and church.

3. What kinds of visits could your church make that would better meet the needs of your members and community?

4. Identify some ways your church can strengthen its visitation ministry. Who should take the lead in encouraging this objective?

5. How well equipped are church members to make the various kinds of visits your church needs to make?

FIVE

Be Equipped: How Should Scripture and Prayer Be Used?

As a teenager I often visited Mrs. McIntire, an older church member who was confined to her home. I have known few Christians as godly as Mrs. McIntire. During each visit, soon after we exchanged greetings, she would say, "Now don't forget, before you leave I want you to read the Bible and have prayer with me." By the time I'd gone on to college she moved into a nursing home. Each time I came back home I would stop by the nursing home to see her. She always greeted me with a bright smile as I gave her a hug. She would remind me that it was my duty to read the Bible and pray with her before I left.

This experience, as well as others in subsequent years, convinced me of the value of using Scripture and prayer in church visitation. Now I routinely ask the persons whom I'm visiting if they would allow me to read the Bible and have prayer with them.

The church visitor should not be expected to know where the Bible speaks to every specific situation one might encounter in church visitation. A good Bible concordance or topical study Bible will help the visitor find Scripture passages that describe principles that apply to each particular person's needs. Since church visitation isn't typically restricted to a single visit, we will likely have other opportunities to follow up with a person. So if he or she raises a question or mentions an issue for which you don't know where to find biblical direction, you can suggest that you'll find the Bible passage and get back to him or her later. You can arrange a convenient time to make a return visit—or you can telephone or e-mail the desired information. Various books are available to help you find Scripture verses that relate to daily needs. These include *God's Answers for Life's Needs*[14] and *Quick Scripture References for Counselors.*[15]

Yet what is needed is more than simply finding the right Scripture passage to meet a particular need. A key to effectively using the Bible and prayer in church visitation is the personal devotional life of the church visitor. Regular and systematic reading and meditating on God's Word and the cultivating of a healthy prayer life enhance the opportunity to use the Bible and prayer in church visitation. Ministry should overflow from our own personal walk with the Lord.

THE SIGNIFICANCE OF THE BIBLE

The Bible has always occupied a special place in the Christian church and in the lives of individual believers. Scripture has been accepted as authoritative by Christians in every century, including the first. Having grown up in a conservative evangelical church, I hold a very high view of the Bible and its importance for one's life. *The Interpreter's Dictionary of the Bible* makes this observation: "Thus, church and Bible are inseparable; there never was a time when the church existed without the Bible or when the church did not acknowledge the author-

---

[14]Paul E. Engle and Margie W. Engle, *God's Answers for Life's Needs* (Grand Rapids: Baker, 2000).

[15]John Kruis, *Quick Scripture References for Counseling* (Grand Rapids: Baker, 2001).

ity of the Bible."[16] The Christian accepts the Bible as a guide for one's life.

Paul in 2 Timothy 3:16–17 identifies the purpose or function that the Bible has for the Christian: "All Scripture is God-breathed and is useful for teaching, rebuking, correcting and training in righteousness, so that the man of God may be thoroughly equipped for every good work."

Paul says that Scripture is God-breathed—inspired—and thus that its message is reliable. But he also identifies it as useful for several purposes:

- ❏ *Teaching.* The Bible should give the Christian knowledge, skill, and instruction in living the godly life.
- ❏ *Rebuking.* Some things in the Christian's life may hinder him or her from being what God wants him or her to be or do. The person may be doing something wrong that needs to be changed. The word *rebuke* means "to criticize or reprove sharply; to reprimand."
- ❏ *Correcting.* Some things in a person's life need to be changed, and some improvements could be made that would bring one's life in harmony with what is described in Scripture.
- ❏ *Training in righteousness.* Christians are called to practice those spiritual disciplines or virtues that help them live lives that please God.

How does the Bible become authoritative for the Christian? As James Barr explains, "The Bible is worthy to be called

---

[16]Alan Richardson, "Authority of Scripture," in *The Interpreter's Dictionary of the Bible* (New York: Abingdon, 1962), 4:248.

Holy Scripture because it conveys, mirrors, or reflects something authentic or valid about God and his works."[17] Wayne Oates observes, "The Bible is a handbook of church and personal discipline, a treasury of ideals of human thought, feelings, and conduct as these experiences are lived out under the rule of God."[18] Scripture reveals how we should relate to God and live our daily lives.

SUGGESTIONS FOR USING THE BIBLE IN CHURCH VISITATION

❏ Read from the Bible in the presence of the one being visited. Even if the verse or passage is one you've memorized, open your Bible and point out the verse as you read it.

❏ Use a modern English translation or paraphrase that will communicate the Bible's message clearly.

❏ Point out the humanness of the biblical characters. The Bible is filled with imperfect people—people like you and me. In spite of the weaknesses and flaws of these people, God forgave their sins and chose to use them for his purposes. There is always hope for us when we confess our sins and seek God's forgiveness.

❏ Speak in a clear, conversational voice. In church visitation you are often in a one-on-one situation, so you should not have to raise or change your voice.

---

[17]James Barr, "Authority of Scripture," in *The Interpreter's Dictionary of the Bible*, supplementary volume (Nashville: Abingdon, 1976), 794.

[18]Wayne E. Oates, *The Bible in Pastoral Care* (Philadelphia: Westminster Press, 1952), 28.

❏ Approach the Bible sincerely with an openness of mind, a fundamental reverence, and a willingness to accept its teaching.

❏ Use the Bible as teaching from God. Scripture is a record of how God has dealt with his people throughout history. It teaches us how we are to relate to God, to the world he created, and to our fellow human beings.

❏ Use the Bible as a means to authenticate the reality of the experience of the persons it describes. It shows people with their strengths and virtues; it also reveals their weaknesses and character flaws. It reveals the depths of degradation to which a person can go and also the heights one can reach through God's power and presence in one's life.

❏ Accept the Bible's message as valid and applicable to life. A proper and positive use of the Bible is stated by the apostle Paul: "For everything that was written in the past was written to teach us, so that through endurance and the encouragement of the Scriptures we might have hope" (Romans 15:4).

HELPFUL PSALMS (AND OTHER PASSAGES) TO USE IN CHURCH VISITATION

Scripture is a treasure-house full of promises and encouraging words appropriate for a variety of life situations. While I couldn't possibly explore all of those situations that might be encountered in visiting with people, let me suggest a couple of psalms I've found to be particularly helpful as I engage in church visitation.

Psalm 46 is so encouraging to someone who is anxious or frightened by what is happening around them. Countless people turned to Psalm 46 after the terrorist attack on the World Trade Center buildings in New York City on September 11, 2001. "Be still and know that God is still God and in control of our world" is the truth revealed in Psalm 46.

Psalm 23 is a favorite Scripture at memorial services. Yet it is much broader in its application, because it can bring comfort whenever and wherever we face the unknown. I found Psalm 23 especially meaningful when I faced heart surgery a few years ago. This psalm points out God's provision for and protection of us in times of need and gives us strength when we feel weak or vulnerable.

I could easily point to other passages, such as Psalms 40, 90, 91, 121, and 139; John 14:1–14; Romans 8:18–39; 2 Corinthians 5:1–10; and Revelation 21:1–5. People involved in visitation, whether seeing someone in a hospital, home, or prison or meeting someone in a restaurant or coffee shop, would do well to have at their fingertips some key passages of Scripture that would be appropriate to use when facing certain common situations.

THINGS TO AVOID IN USING THE BIBLE IN CHURCH VISITATION

❏ Do not state things in a dogmatic, argumentative posture. Let the Bible speak for itself. God's Word does not need us to defend or explain it. Usually there are multiple possible interpretations or applications of biblical truths. Reputable biblical scholars often have different viewpoints as to what a biblical passage means. So visitation is not the best time to get drawn into a heated argument about a difficult passage.

❏ Avoid using the Bible in a legalistic way or as a book of penal discipline. The Bible should never be used as a means to punish or threaten. This misuse of Scripture can often result in people developing a reaction of fear to the Bible. The Bible is a treasury of ideals and resources to equip us to please God and should not be used to pronounce final judgment on the lifestyle of another. Biblical authority should not become a legal justification for one's own merciless judgment of human frailty.[19]

❏ Scripture should not be used to manipulate a person into a decision that one does not understand or will not carry through on.[20] Biblical principles should be shared, but the person must accept them for himself or herself or apply them to his or her own life.

USING PRAYER IN VISITATION

Personal prayer is two-way fellowship and communication with the triune God. We sometimes think of prayer as just asking God for something—to do something we want him to do for us or for those we care about. The dictionary defines prayer as "a reverent petition made to a deity or other object of worship"; "any act of communion with God, such as a confession, praise,

---

[19]See Oates, *The Bible in Pastoral Care,* 29.
[20]See Oates, *The Bible in Pastoral Care,* 39.

or thanksgiving"; "any fervent request." Charles W. F. Smith points out the relationship of the one praying with God's will: "In the Bible prayer moves ... to the heights of spiritual communion and identification of will and activity with God."[21] Our prayer is for God's will to be done in our lives.

It is sometimes difficult to know what we should pray for, especially when visiting with someone who faces a complex life situation. Paul gives us this assurance:

> In the same way, the Spirit helps us in our weakness. We do not know what we ought to pray for, but the Spirit himself intercedes for us with groans that words cannot express. And he who searches our hearts knows the mind of the Spirit, because the Spirit intercedes for the saints in accordance with God's will.

> Romans 8:26–27

During visits I've often wondered what I should pray for, especially if I didn't know the person well. As a young minister I visited a seventeen-year-old boy who had bone cancer, which required amputation of his leg. I don't remember what I said in my prayer, but I recall Barry's words after I finished praying. He angrily said, "It's not *your* leg they're going to cut off." I asked for his forgiveness, and the next morning, prior to his surgery, I prayed, "God, Barry has been in your keeping all his life. As he goes to surgery this morning I pray that your presence will be with him and the surgeons. We commit him into your hands today and in the days ahead."

---

[21]Charles W. F. Smith, "Prayer," in *The Interpreter's Dictionary of the Bible* (Nashville: Abingdon, 1962), 3:857.

We often think that prayer should be spoken and audible. While there are times when it is appropriate to pray audibly, at other times it is best to pray silently. As I visit I pray silently that this visit will accomplish what God wants it to.

Consider also the vast difference between public prayer and private prayer. When I pray in public, I'm aware of the people who are present and their needs. In private prayer I may think of other people, but my prayer is more personal and directed toward my needs or concerns. In private prayer I'm freer to express my feelings, since God (and no one else) hears my prayer. As we pray in church visitation it more closely resembles private prayer. You are aware of the persons you are visiting and what their needs are. Your prayer is between you, the person(s) being visited, and God—and therefore can be more directly targeted to these needs.

SUGGESTIONS FOR USING PRAYER IN CHURCH VISITATION

❏ Use the person's name as you pray. By doing so you personalize the prayer and incorporate him or her into the experience.

❏ Pray in a conversational voice. You are praying with this one person you are visiting, not others who might be in other rooms in the home or nearby (if you are in a public place).

❏ When appropriate ask the person if he or she has any specific ways you might pray for them. Remember to continue praying for these requests in the days following the visit.

❑ Be firmly convinced that God hears our prayers. We can be expectant that God will meet the needs we are praying for.

❑ Be specific as you pray. Pray for healing, strength, power to resist evil, and so forth.

❑ Acknowledge that prayer may be answered immediately or in due time. God answers prayer with three possible responses—yes, no, or not now.

❑ Recognize that different types of prayer are appropriate. Depending on the needs and circumstances, prayer may include or focus specifically on thanksgiving, confession, petition, praise, adoration, intercession, and so forth.

THINGS TO AVOID IN USING PRAYER IN CHURCH VISITATION

❑ Avoid praying in generalities rather than specifics. We often ask God to forgive our sins. We should be specific, asking God to forgive us for losing our temper or for being impatient with a person or a situation.

❑ Do not give false hope. God can and does do miraculous things, yet we cannot tell him what to do or when to do it. We do not know whether God will heal a person, so we should not give false hope.

❑ Avoid using the same type of prayer, regardless of the circumstances. Prayer must be directed to the *specific* needs of people. It may be a prayer of thanksgiving for good things that have happened to the person, or it may be a prayer for strength where a person is weak.

USING PRAYERS FROM SCRIPTURE IN VISITATION

The Bible contains some prayers I've found useful in church visitation. Have you ever tried to repeat Scripture prayers back to the Lord?

For the person who doesn't know how to pray, the model prayer of Jesus in Matthew 6:9–13 would be beneficial:

> This, then, is how you should pray:
>
> "Our Father in heaven,
> hallowed be your name,
> your kingdom come,
> your will be done
> on earth as it is in heaven.
> Give us today our daily bread.
> Forgive us our debts
> as we also have forgiven our debtors.
> And lead us not into temptation,
> but deliver us from the evil one."

For those who need strength and the assurance of God's presence, Ephesians 3:14–21 is especially meaningful:

> For this reason I kneel before the Father, from whom his whole family in heaven and on earth derives its name. I pray that out of his glorious riches he may strengthen you with power through his Spirit in your inner being, so that Christ may dwell in your hearts through faith. And I pray that you, being rooted and established in love, may have power, together with all the saints, to grasp how wide and long and high and

deep is the love of Christ, and to know this love that surpasses knowledge—that you may be filled to the measure of all the fullness of God.

Now to him who is able to do immeasurably more than all we ask or imagine, according to his power that is at work within us, to him be glory in the church and in Christ Jesus throughout all generations, for ever and ever! Amen.

Ephesians 1:16–23 is a prayer of thanksgiving and a petition for God's Spirit and wisdom to reside within us:

I have not stopped giving thanks for you, remembering you in my prayers. I keep asking that the God of our Lord Jesus Christ, the glorious Father, may give you the Spirit of wisdom and revelation, so that you may know him better. I pray also that the eyes of your heart may be enlightened in order that you may know the hope to which he has called you, the riches of his glorious inheritance in the saints, and his incomparably great power for us who believe. That power is like the working of his mighty strength, which he exerted in Christ when he raised him from the dead and seated him at his right hand in the heavenly realms, far above all rule and authority, power and dominion, and every title that can be given, not only in the present age but also in the one to come. And God placed all things under his feet and appointed him to be head over everything for the church, which is his body, the fullness of him who fills everything in every way.

Psalm 63:1–8 is an appropriate prayer for one who is earnestly seeking God and who acknowledges God's presence in his or her life:

O God, you are my God,
  earnestly I seek you;
my soul thirsts for you,
  my body longs for you,
in a dry and weary land
  where there is no water.

I have seen you in the sanctuary
  and beheld your power and your glory.
Because your love is better than life,
  my lips will glorify you.
I will praise you as long as I live,
  and in your name I will lift up my hands.
My soul will be satisfied as with the richest of foods;
  with singing lips my mouth will praise you.

On my bed I remember you;
  I think of you through the watches of the night.
Because you are my help,
  I sing in the shadow of your wings.
My soul clings to you;
  your right hand upholds me.
They who seek my life will be destroyed;
  they will go down to the depths of the earth.
They will be given over to the sword
  and become foods for jackals.

But the king will rejoice in God;
>   all who swear by God's name will praise him,
>   while the mouth of liars will be silenced.

We've now explored together the highlights of the wonderfully rewarding ministry of visitation. While it's impossible to cover every contingency in this short guide, I trust that the territory we've traveled will open your horizons, equip you for effective ministry, and motivate you to remain available for however the Lord may choose to use you with whomever he may send across your path in the days ahead. Armed with the resources of Scripture and prayer, may you draw on the Lord's strength as you serve him with gladness.

QUESTIONS FOR REFLECTION AND DISCUSSION

1. Which Bible passages have been a source of strength and encouragement for you? How did they help you? What is special about these verses for you? Did someone introduce you to these verses?

2. Describe a situation in church visitation when you used the Bible. What worked well with regard to using those particular passages from Scripture?

3. Before you engage in church visitation, how do you prepare yourself? What role do the Bible and prayer play in your preparation?

4. Think about a situation when either your prayer or the prayer of another was particularly meaningful to you. What made this prayer so special?

5. What specific things can your church do to help you and other church visitors more effectively use the Bible and prayer in visitation? Share these ideas with a church leader.

LINCOLN CHRISTIAN COLLEGE AND SEMINARY

108722

ZONDERVAN PRACTICAL MINISTRY GUIDES
Paul E. Engle, Series Editor

SERVING AS A CHURCH GREETER
This practical guidebook will help you reach out to people who need to experience the warmth of belonging to a church family. **Softcover (ISBN 0-310-24764-0).**

SERVING AS A CHURCH USHER
Your impact as an usher is enormous both in meeting the needs of people and in keeping the church service running smoothly. **Softcover (ISBN 0-310-24763-2).**

SERVING IN YOUR CHURCH MUSIC MINISTRY
This wise, concise guidebook will help you harness your God-given musical talent as a gift to the body of Christ. **Softcover (ISBN 0-310-24101-4).**

SERVING BY SAFEGUARDING YOUR CHURCH
Church ought to be the safest place on earth. Here's how to fulfill that goal in practical ways, Includes diagrams, checklists, and resources lists. **Softcover (ISBN 0-310-24105-7).**

SERVING IN CHURCH VISITATION
Whether visiting people in their homes, in the hospital, or in a restaurant over a cup of coffee, the simple act of connecting with others is filled with powerful possibilities. **Softcover (ISBN 0-310-24103-0).**

SERVING IN YOUR CHURCH PRAYER MINISTRY
God moves in praying churches in ways that planning and programs alone can't produce. **Softcover (ISBN 0-310-24758-6).**

SERVING IN YOUR CHURCH NURSERY
Whether you're leading your church's nursery ministry, serving in it, or just thinking of getting involved, you will welcome the expert insights, encouragement, and resources this book offers. **Softcover (ISBN 0-310-24104-9).**

Pick up your copies today at your favorite bookstore!

ZONDERVAN™

GRAND RAPIDS, MICHIGAN 49530 USA

WWW.ZONDERVAN.COM